KILLER PLANTS

SPIKY PLANTS

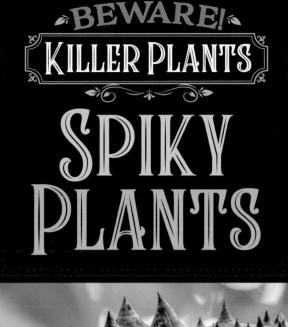

by Joyce Markovics

 CHERRY LAKE PRESS

Ann Arbor, Michigan

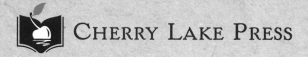

CHERRY LAKE PRESS

Published in the United States of America by Cherry Lake Publishing Group
Ann Arbor, Michigan
www.cherrylakepublishing.com

Reading Adviser: Beth Walker Gambro, MS Ed., Reading Consultant, Yorkville, IL
Content Adviser: Angie Andrade, Senior Horticulturist, Denver Botanic Gardens
Book Designer: Ed Morgan

Photo Credits: © Lucian Coman/Shutterstock, cover and title page; © Nature Picture Library/Jurgen Freund/Alamy Stock Photo, 4; © Dan Campbell/Shutterstock, 5; © chippix/Shutterstock, 6; Dick van Toorn, Wikimedia Commons, 7; © Mortortion Films/Shutterstock, 8; © Ecopix/Shutterstock, 9; © freepik.com, 10; © Bildagentur Zoonar GmbH/Shutterstock, 11; © Slatan/Shutterstock, 12; © freepik.com, 13; © Wasim Muklashy/Shutterstock, 14; © IrinaK/Shutterstock, 15 top; Nebarnix, Wikimedia Commons, 15 bottom; © Jesus Cervantes/Shutterstock, 16–17; © Pat Canova/Alamy Stock Photo, 18; © mikluha_maklai/Shutterstock, 19; © Ian Redding/Shutterstock, 20; © freepik.com, 21 left; © Carlos Leopardi/Shutterstock, 21 right; © Angel DiBilio/Shutterstock, 22.

Cherry Lake Press is an imprint of Cherry Lake Publishing Group.

Library of Congress Cataloging-in-Publication Data

Names: Markovics, Joyce L., author.
Title: Spiky plants / by Joyce Markovics.
Description: Ann Arbor, Michigan : Cherry Lake Publishing, [2021] | Series:
   Beware! killer plants | Includes bibliographical references and index. |
   Audience: Grades 4-6
Identifiers: LCCN 2021001271 (print) | LCCN 2021001272 (ebook) | ISBN
   9781534187719 (hardcover) | ISBN 9781534189119 (paperback) | ISBN
   9781534190511 (pdf) | ISBN 9781534191914 (ebook)
Subjects: LCSH: Poisonous plants—Juvenile literature. | Dangerous
   plants—Juvenile literature.
Classification: LCC QK100.A1 M378 2021 (print) | LCC QK100.A1 (ebook) |
   DDC 581.6/59—dc23
LC record available at https://lccn.loc.gov/2021001271
LC ebook record available at https://lccn.loc.gov/2021001272

Printed in the United States of America
Corporate Graphics

CONTENTS

Stinging Tree

There's a small tree in Australia that sends people screaming in pain. Its fuzzy leaves look harmless. But they are covered with tiny, poison-filled hairs. Each hair is like a very small **hypodermic** needle.

The hairs on the stinging tree's leaves are made from the same material as glass. They can easily get stuck in a person's skin.

The stinging tree grows in forests in northern Australia.

The stinging tree, or gympie, is called the most painful plant in the world. In 1941, a solider fell onto a stinging tree while training. At first, he felt as though he was being stung by a thousand bees. Then his heart began to race. Sweat poured down his face.

WARNING: Plants can be deadly. Never touch or eat an unfamiliar plant.

The soldier was taken to the hospital. He writhed in pain for 3 weeks. The pain was so bad that he had to be tied to his bed! It's the "worst kind of pain you can imagine," said ecologist Marina Hurley.

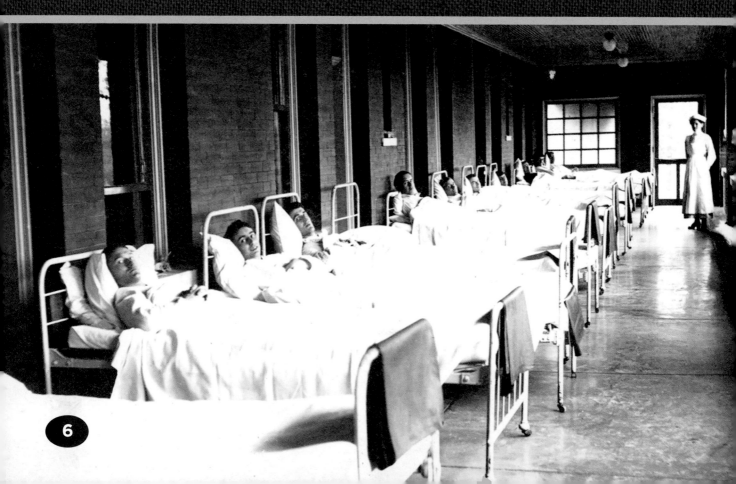

The soldier was taken to a hospital like this one. Months after being stung by the stinging tree, the pain can return. This can happen if the affected area is touched or put in hot or cold water.

It's like "being burnt with hot acid and electrocuted at the same time," said Hurley. The shock of the pain is so great that it has been known to cause heart attacks. "It's 10 times worse than anything else," said another person after being stung by the tree. And the pain can last for months.

The stinging tree produces red fruit that looks like little raspberries. The fruits also contain stinging hairs.

The poison in the tree's hairs, rather than the hairs themselves, causes the severe pain.

When Marina Hurley studies the dangerous tree, she protects herself. She wears heavy gloves and a mask. The stinging tree sheds its poison hairs all the time. As a result, they can land in a person's eyes or enter the lungs.

A scientist in a protective suit carefully examines a plant.

These holes on a stinging tree's leaves were caused by hungry insects.

However, the painful hairs don't stop some animals from feeding on the tree. Hurley has seen insects, frogs, and lizards chewing on the leaves. A kind of wallaby can munch all the leaves off the tree in one night! It's not known if the animals are immune to the poison—or if they can put up with a lot of pain!

Nasty Nettles

The stinging tree is part of the nettle plant family. Nettles are **notorious** for their jagged leaves and stinging hairs. Another kind, the stinging nettle, is widespread in the United States and Europe. The plant can grow up to 4 feet (1.2 meters)—or about as tall as a fourth grader.

Stinging nettle plants

A stinging nettle's needlelike hairs

Covering the nettle's leaves and stem are short, stiff hairs. The hairs contain different chemicals that can irritate the skin. When a person touches the plant, the skin begins to sting and burn. The discomfort usually goes away after 15 minutes.

Scientists think the stinging nettle's hairs are a defense to keep animals from eating it.

Despite their irritating hairs, nettles are sometimes grown in gardens. Why? For hundreds of years, the plant has been used for medicine and food. People enjoy eating nettles in soup or drinking nettle tea.

Nettles should only be handled with thick gloves.

It's best to **harvest** young nettles in the spring. Once picked, the plants must be boiled to remove the hairs. Then the leaves can be made into soup or other dishes. Sometimes, the leaves are brewed to make tea. The tea is used to relieve pain or treat **allergies** like hay fever.

Stinging nettle tea

Spiky Succulents

Other plants also stab and poke. Desert-dwelling cacti are some of the most famous. The jumping cholla is known for jabbing people walking past it.

Cholla cacti

This treelike cactus grows in the southwestern United States. Its stems are covered with big white spines and smaller hairlike spines called glochids. If a person brushes against the cactus, chunks of the plant break off. These pieces grab onto skin or clothing. Then the cactus's sharp spines can pierce the skin.

A piece of a jumping cholla cactus stuck in a person's skin

An up-close look at a cholla spine shows microscopic barbs. These backward-facing barbs are hard to remove from the skin.

The agave is another **succulent** that can draw blood. The plant's leaves have sharp spiked edges. At the end of each leaf tip is a needlelike point. In fact, early people used the points as sewing needles!

The sap of some agave plants can irritate the skin, causing a red, itchy rash.

In 2015, a hiker in Arizona was **impaled** after falling on an agave plant. One agave needle broke off in the man's chest. It caused terrible pain. The agave needle was later removed at a hospital. The hiker won't soon forget being stabbed by a plant.

SINISTER SEEDS

A large shrub grows on the African island of Madagascar. It's prized for its huge yellow flowers. And it's hated for its spiky seedpods. Locals say the seedpods can catch mice. So they call the plant the mousetrap tree.

The mousetrap tree

A mousetrap tree's spiky seedpod

After the shrub flowers, it produces large green fruits. The fruits are covered with small, curved spines that look like fishhooks. As the fruits dry, the spines harden. The dried brown seedpod can hook onto anything, including small animals. It's nearly impossible to remove. The more the seed is pulled, the more the spines grip.

The mousetrap tree can reach a height of 12 feet (3.7 m). The shrub's spiky pods help spread its seeds.

Burrs are plants that also produce prickly seed cases. Once they grab onto you, they never want to let go. Several plants produce burrs. The cocklebur often grows in pastures. The seedpods get stuck in sheep wool, driving farmers crazy.

Burrs stuck in a sheep's wool

The sandbur usually attacks underfoot. When people walk barefoot on the grasslike plant, the spiky burrs can pierce the skin. They can also become stuck inside the mouths of grazing animals. *Ouch!*

A sandbur's prickers

Burdock is another kind of burr. These burrs inspired a Swiss scientist to invent Velcro, a super-strong fastener.

21

PLANT PARTNERS

The whistling thorn acacia tree is covered with big thorns. Each thorn hides an army of stinging ants. First, the ants chew a hole in the thorn and build a nest inside it. When animals try to eat the tree's leaves, the ants sting them. This protects the ants' home and the tree!

Whistling Thorn Acacia Tree

The acacia tree thorns provide a safe home for ants. The tree also makes nectar for the ants to eat.

Acacia Ant

Acacia ants protect acacia trees from hungry animals. They also prune the tree to encourage new growth and kill any seedlings around the tree.

GLOSSARY

allergies (AL-er-jeez) a medical condition that causes someone to become sick after eating, touching, or breathing something that is harmless to most people, such as dog fur

ecologist (ee-KOL-uh-jist) a person who studies the relationships between plants, animals, and their environments

electrocuted (i-LEK-truh-kyoot-id) killed by a strong electric shock

glochids (GLOH-kidz) small hairlike spines on the jumping cholla cactus

harvest (HAR-vist) to collect or gather plants

hypodermic (hye-puh-DUR-mik) introduced under the skin

immune (ih-MYOON) protected from something, such as a poison or disease

impaled (im-PAYLD) injured or killed by piercing with something sharp

microscopic (mye-kruh-SKAH-pik) something so small that it is hard to see without a microscope

nectar (NEK-tur) a sweet liquid produced by plants

notorious (noh-TAWR-ee-uhss) well known for something bad

pastures (PASS-churz) grass-covered fields where animals can graze

succulent (SUHK-yuh-luhnt) a type of plant with thick, fleshy leaves or stems adapted for storing water

wallaby (WOL-uh-bee) an Australian animal that's similar to but smaller than a kangaroo

writhed (RYTHD) twisted in pain

Find Out More

Books

Hirsch, Rebecca E. *When Plants Attack: Strange and Terrifying Plants*. Minneapolis: Millbrook Press, 2019.

Lawler, Janet. *Scary Plants*. New York: Penguin Young Readers, 2017.

Thorogood, Chris. *Perfectly Peculiar Plants*. Lake Forest, CA: Words & Pictures, 2018.

Websites

Brooklyn Botanic Garden: Stinging Nettle
   https://www.bbg.org/gardening/article/stinging_nettle

Pacific Horticulture Society: The Madagascar Spiny Forest at Los Angeles County Arboretum
   https://www.pacifichorticulture.org/articles/the-madagascar-spiny-forestat-los-angeles-county-arboretum/

YouTube: Dr. Marina Hurley and Her Stinging Tree Research
   https://www.youtube.com/watch?v=2VS69FXbjN8

Index

About The Author

Joyce Markovics enjoys writing about and collecting unusual plants. One of her favorites is a mystery orchid that a friend gave to her. She has no idea what the plant's flowers will look like and can't wait to find out.